JOHN LENNON

THE LYRICS OF JOHN LENNON

OMNIBUS PRESS

ISBN 0.7119.6194.8
ORDER NO.OP 47874

EXCLUSIVE DISTRIBUTORS:

BOOK SALES LIMITED,
8-9 FRITH STREET,
LONDON W1V 5TZ, UK.

MUSIC SALES CORPORATION,
257 PARK AVENUE SOUTH,
NEW YORK, NY 10010, USA.

MUSIC SALES PTY LIMITED,
120 ROTHSCHILD AVENUE, ROSEBERY,
NSW 2018, AUSTRALIA.

TO THE MUSIC TRADE ONLY:
MUSIC SALES LIMITED,
8-9 FRITH STREET,
LONDON W1V 5TZ, UK.

COVER AND BOOK DESIGNED BY
PEARCE MARCHBANK, STUDIO TWENTY

PHOTO CREDITS:
COVERS: STARFILE
COVER PHOTOS: BOB GRUEN/STAR FILE.
TEXT PHOTOS SUPPLIED BY HARRY GOODWIN,
BOB GRUEN/STAR FILE, LFI, RETNA AND REX FEATURES.
WHILE EVERY EFFORT HAS BEEN MADE TO TRACE ALL THE COPYRIGHT HOLDERS OF THE PHOTOGRAPHS SOME WERE UNTRACEABLE. PLEASE COULD THOSE CONCERNED CONTACT OMNIBUS PRESS AT 8-9 FRITH STREET, LONDON W1V 5TZ, UK.

THANKS TO ALEXIS ROSENBERG

PRINTED BY PAGE BROS LTD, NORWICH.

A CATALOGUE RECORD FOR THIS BOOK IS AVAILABLE FROM THE BRITISH LIBRARY.

VISIT OMNIBUS PRESS AT
http://www.musicsales.co.uk

Cold Turkey
Words and music by John Lennon

Give Peace A Chance
Words and music by John Lennon and Paul McCartney

God
Hold On
I Found Out
Isolation
Look At Me
Mother
My Mummy's Dead
Remember
Well Well Well
Working Class Hero
Words and music by John Lennon

Instant Karma
Words and music by John Lennon

Imagine
Jealous Guy
Love
Oh Yoko
Power To The People
Words and music by John Lennon

Happy Xmas (War Is Over)
Words and music by John Lennon andYoko Ono

Crippled Inside
Gimme Some Truth
How?
How Do You Sleep?
I Don't Wanna Be A Soldier
It's So Hard
Words and music by John Lennon

John Sinclair
New York City
Words and music by John Lennon

Angela
Attica State
The Luck Of The Irish
Sunday Bloody Sunday
Woman Is The Nigger Of The World
Words and Music by John Lennon andYoko Ono

Scumbag
Words and music by John Lennon, Yoko Ono andFrank Zappa

Aisumasen (I'm Sorry)
Bring On The Lucie (Freeda Peeple)
I Know (I Know)
Intuition
Meat City
Mind Games
Nobody Loves You (When You Are Down And Out)
One Day At A Time
Only People
Out The Blue
Rock'N'Roll People
Tight A$
You Are Here
Words and music by John Lennon

Oh My Love
Words and music by John Lennon and Yoko Ono

Bless You
Going Down On Love
Move Over Ms.L
Scared
Steel & Glass
Surprise Surprise
Whatever Gets You Through The Night
What You Got
Words and music by John Lennon

Old Dirt Road
Words and music by John Lennon and Harry Nilsson

#9 Dream
Words and music by John Lennon

Beautiful Boy (Darling Boy)
Clean Up Time
Dear Yoko
(Just Like) Starting Over
I'm Losing You
Watching The Wheels
Woman
Words and music by John Lennon

DISCOGRAPHY

SINGLES

Give Peace A Chance
Remember Love
APPLE 13. UK RELEASE: JULY 1969.

Cold Turkey
Don't Worry Kyoko (Mummy's Only Looking For Her Hand In The Snow)
APPLE 1001. UK RELEASE: OCTOBER 1969.

Instant Karma!
Who Has Seen The Wind
APPLE 1003. UK RELEASE: FEBRUARY 1970.

Mother
Why?
APPLE 1827. US RELEASE: DECEMBER 1970.

Power To The People
Open Your Box
APPLE R 5892. UK RELEASE: MARCH 1971.

Power To The People
Touch Me
APPLE 1830. US RELEASE: MARCH 1971.

Imagine
It's So Hard
APPLE 1840. US RELEASE: OCTOBER 1971.

Happy Xmas (War Is Over)
Listen The Snow Is Falling
APPLE R 5970. UK RELEASE: NOVEMBER 1972.

Woman Is The Nigger Of The World
Sisters O Sisters
APPLE 1848. US RELEASE: APRIL 1972.

Mind Games
Meat City
APPLE R 5994. UK RELEASE: NOVEMBER 1973.

Whatever Gets You Thru The Night
Beef Jerky
APPLE R 5998. UK RELEASE: OCTOBER 1974.

#9 Dream
What You Got
APPLE R 6003. UK RELEASE: JANUARY 1975.

Stand By Me
Move Over Ms L
APPLE R 6005. UK RELEASE: APRIL 1975.

Imagine
Working Class Hero
APPLE 6009. UK RELEASE: OCTOBER 1975.

(Just Like) Starting Over
Kiss Kiss Kiss
GEFFEN K 79186. UK RELEASE: OCTOBER 1980.

Woman
Beautiful Boys
GEFFEN K 79185. UK RELEASE: JANUARY 1981.

Watching The Wheels
I'm Your Angel
GEFFEN K79207. UK RELEASE: MARCH 1981.

Love
Gimme Some Truth
PARLOPHONE R 6059. UK RELEASE: NOVEMBER 1982.

Nobody Told Me
O Sanity
POLYDOR POSP 700. UK RELEASE: JANUARY 1984.

Borrowed Time
Your Hands
POLYDOR POSP 701. UK RELEASE: MARCH 1984.

Borrowed Time
Your Hands
Never Say Goodbye
POLYDOR POSPX 701. UK RELEASE: MARCH 1984.

Give Peace A Chance
Cold Turkey
EMI G45 2. UK RELEASE: MARCH 1984.

I'm Stepping Out
Sleepless Night
POLYDOR POSP 702. UK RELEASE JULY 1984.

I'm Stepping Out
Sleepless Night
Loneliness
POLYDOR POSPX 702. UK RELEASE: JULY 1984.

Every Man Has A Woman Who Loves Him
It's Alright
POLYDOR POSP 712. UK RELEASE: NOVEMBER 1984.

Jealous Guy
Going Down On Love
PARLOPHONE R 6117. UK RELEASE: NOVEMBER 1985.

Jealous Guy
Going Down On Love
Oh Yoko!
PARLOPHONE 12R 6117. UK RELEASE: NOVEMBER 1985.

Jealous Guy
Give Peace A Chance
CAPITOL B 442230. UK RELEASE: SEPTEMBER 1988.

Imagine
Jealous Guy
PARLOPHONE R 6199. UK RELEASE: DECEMBER 1988.

Imagine
Jealous Guy
Happy Xmas (War Is Over)
PARLOPHONE 12R 6199. UK RELEASE: DECEMBER 1988.

Imagine
Jealous Guy
Happy Xmas (War Is Over)
Give Peace A Chance
PARLOPHONE CDR 6119. UK RELEASE: DECEMBER 1988.

ALBUMS

Unfinished Music No.1: Two Virgins
UK RELEASE: NOVEMBER 1968
(ORIGINAL UK ISSUE: APPLE (S)APCOR 2)

Unfinished Music No.2: Life With The Lions
UK RELEASE: MAY 1969
(ORIGINAL UK ISSUE: ZAPPLE 01)

Wedding Album
UK RELEASE: NOVEMBER 1969
(ORIGINAL UK ISSUE: SAPCOR 13)

Live Peace In Toronto 1969
UK RELEASE: DECEMBER 1969
(ORIGINAL UK ISSUE: APPLE CORE 2001)

John Lennon / Plastic Ono Band
UK RELEASE: DECEMBER 1970
(ORIGINAL UK ISSUE: APPLE PCS 7124)

Imagine
UK RELEASE: OCTOBER 1971
(ORIGINAL UK ISSUE: APPLE SAPCOR 10004)

Sometime In New York City
UK RELEASE: JUNE 1972 (US) SEPTEMBER 1972 (UK)
(ORIGINAL UK ISSUE: APPLE PCSP 716)

Mind Games
UK RELEASE: NOVEMBER 1973
(ORIGINAL UK ISSUE: APPLE PCS 7165)

Walls And Bridges
UK RELEASE: OCTOBER 1974
(ORIGINAL UK ISSUE: APPLE PCTC 254)

Rock'n'roll
UK RELEASE: FEBRUARY 1975
(ORIGINAL UK ISSUE: APPLE PCS 7169)

Shaved Fish
UK RELEASE: OCTOBER 1975
(ORIGINAL UK ISSUE: APPLE PCS 7173)

Double Fantasy
UK RELEASE: NOVEMBER 1980
(ORIGINAL UK ISSUE: GEFFEN K 99131)

POSTHUMOUS RELEASES

The John Lennon Collection
UK RELEASE: NOVEMBER 1982
(ORIGINAL UK ISSUE: PARLOPHONE EMTV 37]

Heart Play: An Unfinished Dialogue
UK RELEASE: DECEMBER 1983
(ORIGINAL UK ISSUE: POLYDOR 817 238-1]

Milk And Honey: A Heart Play
UK RELEASE: JANUARY 1984
(ORIGINAL UK ISSUE: POLYDOR POLH 5]

Live In New York City
UK RELEASE: FEBRUARY 1986
(ORIGINAL UK ISSUE: PARLOPHONE PCS 7301]

Menlove Avenue
UK RELEASE: OCTOBER 1986
(ORIGINAL UK ISSUE: PARLOPHONE PCS 7308]

Imagine: John Lennon
UK RELEASE: OCTOBER 1988
(ORIGINAL UK ISSUE: PARLOPHONE PCSP 722]

Lennon
UK RELEASE: OCTOBER 1990
(ORIGINAL UK ISSUE: PARLOPHONE CDS 79 5220 2]

LYRICS

GIVE PEACE A CHANCE

Everybody's talking about...
Bagism,
Shagism,
Dragism,
Madism,
Ragism,
Tagism,
Thisism,
Thatism,
Isn't it the most?

All we are saying
Is give peace a chance
All we are saying
Is give peace a chance

Everybody's talking about...
Ministers
Sinisters
Bannisters
And canisters
Bishops
And Fishops
Rabbis
And Popeyes
Bye bye, bye byes

All we are saying
Is give peace a chance
All we are saying
Is give peace a chance

Everybody's talking about...
Revolution
Evolution
Masturbation
Flagellations
Regulations
Integrations
Meditation
United Nations
Congratulations

All we are saying
Is give peace a chance
All we are saying
Is give peace a chance

Everybody's talking about...
John and Yoko
Timmy Leary
Rosemary
Tommy Smothers
Bobby Dylan
Tommy Cooper
Derek Taylor
Norman Mailer
Allen Ginsberg
Hare Krishna
Hare hare Krishna

All we are saying
Is give peace a chance
All we are saying
Is give peace a chance

COLD TURKEY

Temperature's rising fever is high
Can't see no future can't see no sky
My feet are so heavy, so is my head
I wish I was a baby, I wish I was dead

Cold turkey has got me on the run (ah)

My body is aching goose-pimple bone
Can't see nobody, leave me alone
My eyes are wide open, can't get to sleep
One thing I'm sure of I'm in at the deep freeze

Cold turkey has got me on the run (ah) Ah
Oh Oo Oh
Cold turkey has got me on the run

Thirty six hours rolling in pain
Praying to someone free me again
Oh I'll be a good boy, please make me well
I promise you anything, get me out of this hell

Cold turkey has got me on the run (ah)
Oh Oo No Oh Oo No . . .

HAIR
PEACE.

INSTANT KARMA

Instant Karma's gonna get you
Gonna knock you right on the head
You better get yourself together
Pretty soon, you're gonna be dead
What in the world you thinking of
Laughing in the face of love?
What on earth you tryin' to do?
It's up to you, yeah you

Instant Karma's gonna get you
Gonna look you right in the face
You better get yourself together darlin'
Join the human race
How in the world you gonna see
Laughin' at fools like me?
Who in the hell d'you think you are?
A superstar?
Well, alright you are
Well we all shine on
Like the moon and the stars and the sun
Well we all shine on
Ev'ryone come on

Instant Karma's gonna get you
Gonna knock you off your feet
Better recognise your brothers
Ev'ryone you meet
Why in the world are we here?
Surely not to live in pain and fear
Why on earth are you there?
When you're ev'rywhere
Come and get your share

Well we all shine on
Like the moon and the stars and the sun
Well we all shine on
Come on and on and on on
Yeah yeah alright ah ah

Well we all shine on
Like the moon and the stars and the sun
Well we all shine on
Come on and on and on

Well we all shine on
Like the moon and the stars and the sun
Well we all shine on

POWER TO THE PEOPLE

Power to the people
Power to the people
Power to the people
Power to the people
Power to the people
Power to the people
Power to the people
Power to the people right on

You say you want a revolution,
We'd better get it on right away
Well let's get on your feet,
Into the street, singing

Power to the people
Power to the people
Power to the people
Power to the people
Power to the people
Power to the people
Power to the people
Power to the people right on

A million workers workin' for nothing,
You'd better give them what they really own
We gotta put you down when we come in to town, singing

Power to the people
Power to the people
Power to the people
Power to the people
Power to the people
Power to the people
Power to the people
Power to the people right on

I gonna ask you comrades and brothers,
How do you treat your old woman back home
She's gotta be herself so she can give us help, singing

Power to the people
Power to the people...
Power to the people right on

HAPPY XMAS (WAR IS OVER)

So this is Xmas and what have you done?
Another year over, a new one just begun

And so this is Xmas, I hope you have fun
The near and the dear ones, the old and the young

A merry merry Xmas and a happy New Year,
Let's hope it's a good one without any fear

And so this is Xmas for weak and for strong
The rich and the poor ones, the road is so long.
(War is over if you want it, war is over now)

And so happy Xmas for black and for white
For the yellow and red ones let's stop all the fights.
(War is over if you want it, war is over now)

A merry merry Xmas and a Happy New Year,
Let's hope it's a good one without any fear

And so this is Xmas and what have we done?
Another year over, a new one just begun

And so happy Xmas, we hope you have fun
The near and the dear ones, the old and the young

A merry merry Xmas and a happy New Year,
Let's hope it's a good one without any fear

War is over if you want it, war is over now

MOTHER

Mother, you had me but I never had you
I wanted you, you didn't want me
So I, I just got to tell you goodbye, goodbye

Father, you left me but I never left you
I needed you, you didn't need me
So I, I just got to tell you goodbye, goodbye

Children, don't do what I have done
I couldn't walk and I tried to run
So I, I just got to tell you goodbye, goodbye

Mama don't go, Daddy come home
Mama don't go, Daddy come home

HOLD ON

Hold on John
John hold on
It's gonna be alright
You're gonna win the fight

Hold on Yoko
Yoko hold on
It's gonna be alright
You're gonna make the flight

When you're by yourself
And there's no one else
You'll just have yourself
And you'll tell yourself
Just to hold on

Hold on World
World hold on
It's gonna be alright
You're gonna see the light
And when you're one
Really one
Well you get things done
Like they've never been done
So hold on

I FOUND OUT

I told you before stay away from my door,
Don't give me that brother, brother, brother, brother;
The freaks on the phone won't leave me alone,
So don't give me that brother brother brother, brother, No!

I, I found out
I, I found out

Now that I showed you what I been through
Don't take nobody's word what you can do
There ain't no Jesus gonna come from the sky
Now that I found out I know I can cry

I, I found out
I, I found out

Some of you sitting there with your cock in your hand
Don't get you nowhere don't make you a man
I heard something 'bout my Ma and my Pa
They didn't want me so they made me a star

I, I found out
I, I found out

Old Hare Krishna got nothing on you
Just keep you crazy with nothing to do
Keep you occupied with pie in the sky
There ain't no Guru who can see through your eyes

I, I found out
I, I found out

I seen through junkies, I been through it all
I seen religion from Jesus to Paul
Don't let them fool you with dope and cocaine
No one can harm you, feel your own pain

I found out! Ah, Ah

WORKING CLASS HERO

As soon as you're born they make you feel small
By giving you no time instead of it all
Till the pain is so big you feel nothing at all

A working class hero is something to be
A working class hero is something to be

They hurt you at home and they hit you at school
They hate you if you're clever and they despise a fool
Till you're so fucking crazy you can't follow their rules

A working class hero is something to be
A working class hero is something to be

When they've tortured and scared you for 20 odd years
Then they expect you to pick a career
When you can't really function you're so full of fear

A working class hero is something to be
A working class hero is something to be

Keep you doped with religion and sex and TV
And you think you're so clever and classless and free
But you're still fucking peasants as far as I can see

A working class hero is something to be
A working class hero is something to be

There's room at the top they are telling you still
But first you must learn how to smile as you kill
If you want to be like the folks on the hill

A working class hero is something to be
A working class hero is something to be

Keep you doped with religion and sex and t.v.
And you think you're so clever and classless and free
But you're still fucking peasants as far as I can see

A working class hero is something to be
A working class hero is something to be
If you want to be a hero well just follow me
If you want to be a hero well just follow me

ISOLATION

People say we got it made
Don't they know we're so afraid?
Isolation
We're afraid to be alone
Everybody got to have a home
Isolation

Just a boy and a little girl
trying to change the whole wide world
Isolation
The world is just a little town
Everybody trying to put us down
I - Isolation

I don't expect you to understand after you caused so much pain
But then again you're not to blame,
You're just a human, a victim of the insane

We're afraid of everyone, afraid of the sun
Isolation
The sun will never disappear, but the world may not have many years
I - Isolation

REMEMBER

Remember when you were young
How the hero was never hung
Always got away
Remember how the man
Used to leave you empty handed
Always, always let you down
If you ever change your mind
About leaving it all behind
Remember, remember today

Hey, don't feel sorry 'bout the way it's gone
Don't you worry 'bout what you've done

Remember when you were small
How people seemed so tall.
Always had their way, hey, hey.
Do you remember your ma and pa
Just wishing for movie stardom.
Always, always playing a part
If you ever feel so sad
And the whole world is driving you mad
Remember, remember today

Hey, don't feel sorry 'bout the way it's gone
Don't you worry 'bout what you've done
No, remember,
Remember the Fifth of November

LOVE

Love is real, real is love
Love is feeling, feeling love.
Love is wanting to be loved.

Love is touch, touch is love
Love is reaching, reaching love.
Love is asking to be loved

Love is you, you and me
Love is knowing we can be

Love is free, free is love
Love is living, living love.
Love is needing to be loved

WELL WELL WELL

Well, well, well oh well
Well, well, well oh well

I took my loved one out to dinner
So we could get a bite to eat
And though we both had been much thinner
She looked so beautiful I could eat her

Well, well, well oh well
Well, well, well oh well

I took my loved one to a big field
So we could watch the English sky
We both were nervous, feeling guilty
And neither one of us knew just why

Well, well, well oh well
Well, well, well oh well

We sat and talked of revolution
Just like two liberals in the sun.
We talked of women's liberation
And how the hell we could get things done

Well, well, well oh well
Well, well, well oh well

Well, well, well oh well
Well, well, well oh well

Well, well, well, well, well, well, well
Well, well, well, well, well, well, well

LOOK AT ME

Look at me, who am I supposed to be?
Who am I supposed to be?
Look at me, what am I supposed to be?
What am I supposed to be?
Look at me, Oh my love
Oh, my love

Here I am what am I supposed to do?
What am I supposed to do?
Here I am, what can I do for you?
What can I do for you
Here I am, Oh my love, Oh my love
Look at me, oh please look at me, my love
Here I am, oh my love

Who am I? Nobody knows but me
Nobody knows but me
Who am I? Nobody else can see
Just you and me
Who are we?
Oh my Love, Oh my Love

GOD

God is a concept by which we measure our pain
I'll say it again
God is a concept by which we measure our pain
Yeah, pain yeah, pain

I don't believe in magic
I don't believe in I Ching
I don't believe in Bible
I don't believe in Tarot
I don't believe in Hitler
I don't believe in Jesus
I don't believe in Kennedy
I don't believe in Buddha
I don't believe in Mantra
I don't believe in Gita
I don't believe in Yoga
I don't believe in Kings
I don't believe in Elvis
I don't believe in Zimmerman
I don't believe in Beatles

I just believe in me Yoko and me
And that's reality

The dream is over, what can I say
The dream is over yesterday

I was the dream weaver but now I'm reborn
I was the walrus but now I'm John
And so dear friends you'll just have to carry on
The dream is over

MY MUMMY'S DEAD

My Mummy's dead
I can't get it through my head
Though it's been so many years
My Mummy's dead
I can't explain so much pain
I could never show it
My Mummy's dead

IMAGINE

Imagine there's no heaven
It's easy if you try
No hell below us
Above us only sky

Imagine all the people
Living for today
Aha

Imagine there's no country
It isn't hard to do
Nothing to kill or die for
And no religion too

Imagine all the people
Living life in peace
Yoo-hoo

You may say that I'm a dreamer
But I'm not the only one
I hope some day you'll join us
And the world will be as one

Imagine no possessions
I wonder if you can
No need for greed or hunger
A brotherhood of man

Imagine all the people
Sharing all the world
Yoo-hoo

You may say that I'm a dreamer
But I'm not the only one
I hope some day you'll join us
And the world will live as one

CRIPPLED INSIDE

You can shine your shoes and wear a suit
You can comb your hair and look quite cute
You can hide your face behind a smile
One thing you can't hide is when you're crippled inside

You can wear a mask and paint your face
You can call yourself the human race
You can wear a collar and a tie
One thing you can't hide is when you're crippled inside

Well now you know that your cat has nine lives babe
Nine lives to itself
You only got one and a dog's life ain't fun
Mamma take a look outside

You can go to church and sing a hymn
You can judge me by the colour of my skin
You can live a lie until you die
One thing you can't hide is when you're crippled inside

Well now you know that your cat has nine lives babe
Nine lives to itself
You only got one and a dog's life ain't fun
Mamma take a look outside

You can go to church and sing a hymn
You can judge me by the colour of my skin
You can live a lie until you die
One thing you can't hide is when you're crippled inside

One thing you can't hide is when you're crippled inside

One thing you can't hide is when you're crippled inside

JEALOUS GUY

I was dreaming of the past
And my heart was beating fast
I began to lose control
I began to lose control

I didn't mean to hurt you
I'm sorry that I made you cry
Oh my I didn't mean to hurt you
I'm just a jealous guy

I was feeling insecure
You might not love me anymore
I was shivering inside
I was shivering inside

I didn't mean to hurt you
I'm sorry that I made you cry
Oh my I didn't mean to hurt you
I'm just a jealous guy

I didn't mean to hurt you
I'm sorry that I made you cry
Oh my I didn't mean to hurt you
I'm just a jealous guy

I was trying to catch your eyes
Thought that you was trying to hide
I was swallowing my pain
I was swallowing my pain

I didn't mean to hurt you
I'm sorry that I made you cry
Oh my I didn't mean to hurt you
I'm just a jealous guy - watch out
I'm just a jealous guy - look out babe
I'm just a jealous guy

IT'S SO HARD

You got to live
You got to love
You got to be somebody
You got to shove

But it's so hard
But it's really hard
Sometimes I feel like going down

You got to eat
You got to drink
You got to feel something
You got to worry

But it's so hard
But it's really hard
Sometimes I feel like going down

But when it's good it's really good
And when I hold you in my arms baby
Sometimes I feel like going down

You got to run
You got to hide
You got to keep your woman satisfied

But it's so hard
But it's really hard
Sometimes I feel like going down

I DON'T WANNA BE A SOLDIER

Well I don't wanna be a soldier mama I don't wanna die
Well I don't wanna be a sailor mama I don't wanna fly
Well I don't wanna be a failure mama I don't wanna cry
Well I don't wanna be a soldier mama I don't wanna die
Oh no, Oh no, Oh no, Oh no

Well I don't wanna be a rich man mama I don't wanna cry
Well I don't wanna be a poor man mama I don't wanna fly
Well I don't wanna be a lawyer mama I don't wanna lie
Well I don't wanna be a soldier mama I don't wanna die
Oh no, Oh no, Oh no, Oh no

Well I don't wanna be a beggar mama I don't wanna die
Well I don't wanna be a thief now mama I don't wanna fly
Well I don't wanna be a church man mama I don't wanna cry
Well I don't wanna be a soldier mama I don't wanna die
Oh no, Oh no, Oh no, Oh no, Hey

GIMME SOME TRUTH

I'm sick and tired of hearing things from up-tight
short-sighted narrow-minded hypocrites
All I want is the truth
Just gimme some truth

I've had enough of reading things by neurotic psychotic
pig-headed politicians
All I want is the truth
Just gimme some truth - (now)

No short haired yellow bellied son of tricky Dicky's gonna
Mother Hubbard soft soap me with just a pocket full of hope
(It's) money for dope money for rope

No short haired yellow bellied son of tricky Dicky's gonna
Mother Hubbard soft soap me with just a pocket full of hope
(It's) money for dope money for rope

I'm sick to death of seeing things from tight-lipped condescending
mommies' little chauvinists
All I want is the truth
Just gimme some truth now

I've had enough of watching scenes of schizophrenic egocentric
paranoic primadonnas
All I want is the truth
Just gimme some truth

No short haired yellow bellied son of tricky Dicky's gonna
Mother Hubbard soft soap me with just a pocket full of hope
(It's) money for dope money for rope

I'm sick and tired of hearing things from up-tight short-sighted
narrow-minded hypocrites
All I want is the truth
Just gimme some truth

OH MY LOVE

Oh my love for the first time in my life my eyes are wide open
Oh my lover for the first time in my life my eyes can see
I see the wind, Oh I see the trees
Everything is clear in my heart
I see the clouds, Oh I see the sky
Everything is clear in our world

Oh my love for the first time in my life my mind is wide open
Oh my lover for the first time in my life my mind can feel
I feel sorrow, Oh I feel dreams
Everything is clear in my heart
I feel life, Oh I feel love
Everything is clear in our world.

HOW DO YOU SLEEP?

So Sergeant Pepper took you by surprise
You better see right through that mother's eyes
Those freaks was right when they said you was dead
The one mistake you made was in your head

Oh how do you sleep?
Oh how do you sleep at night?

You live with straights who tell you you was king
Jump when your momma tell you anything
The only thing you done was yesterday
And since you've gone you're just another day

Oh how do you sleep?
Oh how do you sleep at night?

A pretty face may last a year or two
But pretty soon they'll see what you can do
The sound you make is muzak to my ears
You must have learned something in all those years

Oh how do you sleep?
Oh how do you sleep at night?

HOW?

How can I go forward when I don't know which way I'm facing?
How can I go forward when I don't which way to turn?
How can I go forward into something I'm not sure of?
Oh no, Oh no

How can I have feeling when I don't know if it's a feeling?
How can I feel something if I just don't know how to feel?
How can I have feelings when my feelings have always been denied?
Oh no, Oh no

You know life can be long and you got to be so strong
and the world is so tough
Sometimes I feel I've had enough

How can I give love when I don't know what it is I'm giving?
How can I give love when I just don't know how to give?
How can I give love when love is something I ain't never had?
Oh no, Oh no

You know life can be long and you got to be so strong
and the world she's so tough
Sometimes I feel I've had enough

How can we go forward when we don't know which way we're facing?
How can we go forward when we don't know which way to turn?
How can we go forward into something we're not sure of?
Oh no, Oh no.

OH YOKO

In the middle of the night
In the middle of the night I call your name.
Oh Yoko
Oh Yoko
My love will turn you on

In the middle of a bath
In the middle of a bath I call your name
Oh Yoko
Oh Yoko
My love will turn you on
My love will turn you on

In the middle of a shave
In the middle of a shave I call your name
Oh Yoko
Oh Yoko
My love will turn you on

In the middle of a dream
In the middle of a dream I call your name
Oh Yoko
Oh Yoko
My love will turn you on
My love will turn you on

In the middle of a cloud
In the middle of a cloud I call your name
Oh Yoko
Oh Yoko
My love will turn you on
Oh Yoko

WOMAN IS THE NIGGER OF THE WORLD

Woman is the nigger of the World
Yes she is...think about it
Woman is the nigger of the World
Think about it...do something about it.

We make her paint her face and dance
If she won't be a slave we say that she don't love us
If she's real we say she's trying to be a man
While putting her down we pretend that she's above us

Woman is the nigger of the World...yes she is
If you don't believe me take a look at the one you're with
Woman is the slave of the slaves
Ah, yes...better scream about it.

We make her bear and raise our children
And then we leave her flat for being a fat old mother hen
We tell her home is the only place she should be
Then we complain that she's too unworldly to be our friend

Woman is the nigger of the world...yes she is
If you don't believe me take a look at the one you're with
Woman is the slave to the slaves
Yeh (think about it)

We insult her every day on TV
And wonder why she has no guts or confidence
When she's young we kill her will to be free
While telling her not to be so smart we put her down for being so dumb

Woman is the nigger of the World
Yes she is...If you don't believe me take a look at the one you're with
Woman is the slave to the slaves
Yes she is...if you believe me, you better scream about it.

We make her paint her face and dance
We make her paint her face and dance
We make her paint her face and dance

ATTICA STATE

What a waste of human power
What a waste of human lives
Shoot the prisoners in the tower
Forty-three poor widowed wives

Media blames it on the prisoners
But the prisoners did not kill
'Rockefeller pulled the trigger'
That is what the people feel

Attica State, Attica State, we're all mates with Attica State

Free the prisoners, free the judges
Free all prisoners everywhere
All they want is truth and justice
All they need is love and care

They all live in suffocation
Let's not watch them die in sorrow
Now's the time for revolution
Give them all a chance to grow

Attica State, Attica State, we're all mates with Attica State

Come together, join the movement
Take a stand for human rights
Fear and hatred clouds our judgement
Free us all from endless night

Attica State, Attica State, we're all mates with Attica State
Attica State, Attica State, we all live in Attica State.

NEW YORK CITY

Standing on the corner
Just me and Yoko Ono
We was waiting for Jerry to land
Up come a man with a guitar in his hand
Singing 'Have a marijuana if you can'
His name was David Peel
And we found that he was real
He sang 'The Pope smokes dope every day'
Up come a Policeman and shoved us up the street
Singing 'Power to the people today!'
New York City...New York City...New York City...
Que pasa, New York? Que pasa, New York?

Well we went to Max's City
Got down the nitty gritty
With the Elephants Memory Band
Laid something down
As the news spread around
About the Plastic Ono Elephants Memory Band!
Well we played some funky boogie
And laid some tutti frutti
Singing 'Long tall Sally's a man.'
Up come a preacherman trying to be a teacher
Singing 'God's a red herring in drag!'
New York City...Que pasa, New York?

Well we did the Staten Island Ferry
Making movies for the telly
Played the Fillmore and Apollo for freedom,
Tried to shake our image
Just a cycling through the village
But we found out we had left it back in London
Well nobody came to bug us
Hustle us or shove us
So we decided to make it our home
If the man wants to shove us out
We gonna jump and shout
The Statue of Liberty said 'Come!'
New York City...Que pasa, New York?
New York City, down in the Village
What a bad-ass city!
Que pasa, New York? Que pasa, New York?

SUNDAY BLOODY SUNDAY

Well it was Sunday bloody Sunday when they shot the people there
The cries of thirteen martyrs filled the free Derry air
Is there anyone amongst you dare to blame it on the kids?
Not a soldier boy was bleeding when they nailed the coffin lids!

Sunday bloody Sunday,

Bloody Sunday's the day!

You claim to be majority, well you know that it's a lie
You're really a minority on this sweet emerald isle
When Stormont bans our marches, they've got a lot to learn
Internment is no answer, it's those mothers' turn to burn
Sunday bloody Sunday
Bloody Sunday's the day!

You Anglo pigs and Scotties sent to colonise the North
You wave your bloody union jacks and you know what it's worth
How dare you hold to ransom a people proud and free
Keep Ireland for the Irish, put the English back to sea

Sunday bloody Sunday
Bloody Sunday's the day!

It's always bloody Sunday in the concentration camps
Keep Falls Road free forever from the bloody English hands
Repatriate to Britain all of you who call it home
Leave Ireland to the Irish, not for London or for Rome!

Sunday bloody Sunday
Bloody Sunday's the day!
Sunday bloody Sunday
Bloody Sunday's the day!

THE LUCK OF THE IRISH

If you had the luck of the Irish,
You'd be sorry and wish you were dead
You should have the luck of the Irish
And you'd wish you was English instead!

A thousand years of torture and hunger
Drove the people away from their land
A land full of beauty and wonder
Was raped by the British brigands! Goddamn!
Goddamn!

If you could keep voices like flowers
There'd be shamrocks all over the world
If you could drink dreams like Irish streams
Then the world would be high as the Mountain of Morn.

In the 'Pool they told us the story
How the English divided the land.
Of the pain, the death and the glory
And the poets of auld Eireland.

If we could make chains with the morning dew
The world would be like Galway Bay.
Let's walk over rainbows like leprechauns,
The world would be one big blarney stone.

Why the hell are the English there anyway?
As they kill with God on their side!
Blame it all on the kids and the IRA!
As the bastards commit genocide Aye! Aye! Genocide!

If you had the luck of the Irish,
You'd be sorry and wish you were dead
You should have the luck of the Irish
And you'd wish you was English instead!
Yes you'd wish you was English instead!

JOHN SINCLAIR

It ain't fair, John Sinclair
In the stir for breathing air
Won't you care for John Sinclair
In the stir for breathing air?
Let him be
Set him free,
Let him be like you and me.

They gave him ten for two,
What else can the judges do?
We gotta, gotta, gotta, gotta, gotta, gotta, gotta, gotta, gotta, gotta,
gotta, gotta, gotta, gotta, gotta set him free.

If he'd been a soldier man
Shooting gooks in Vietnam
If he was the CIA
Selling dope and making hay
He'd be free they'd let him be
Breathing air like you and me, right on

They gave him ten for two
What else can the judges do?
We gotta, gotta, gotta, gotta, gotta, gotta, gotta, gotta, gotta, gotta,
gotta, gotta, gotta, gotta, gotta set him free.

They gave him ten for two
They got old Lee Otis too
We gotta, gotta, gotta, gotta, gotta, gotta, gotta, gotta, gotta, gotta,
gotta, gotta, gotta, gotta, gotta set him free.

Was he jailed for what he done
Representing every one?
Free John now, if we can,
From the clutches of the man
Let him be, lift the lid
Bring him to his wife and kids

They gave him ten for two
What else can the bastards do?
We gotta, gotta, gotta, gotta, gotta, gotta, gotta, gotta, gotta, gotta,
gotta, gotta, gotta, gotta, gotta set him free.

ANGELA

Angela, they put you in prison
Angela, they shot down your man
Angela, you're one of the millions of political prisoners in the world.

Sister, there's a wind that never dies
Sister, we're breathing together
Sister, our love and hopes forever keep on moving oh so slowly in the world.

They gave you sunshine
They gave you sea
They gave you everything but the jailhouse key.
They gave you coffee
They gave you tea
They gave you everything but equality

Angela, can you hear the earth is turning?
Angela, the world watches you
Angela, you soon will be returning to your sisters and brothers of the world.

They gave you sunshine
They gave you sea
They gave you everything but the jailhouse key.
They gave you coffee
They gave you tea
They gave you everything but equality

Sister, you're still a people teacher
Sister, your word reaches far
Sister, there's a million different races but we all share the same future in the world.

They gave you sunshine
They gave you sea
They gave you everything but the jailhouse key.
They gave you coffee
They gave you tea
They gave you everything but equality

SCUMBAG

Scumbag, Scumbag
Scumbag, Scumbag
Scumbag, Scumbag
Scumbag, Scumbag
You can all sing along to this one coz there's only one word
Scumbag, Scumbag
Scumbag, Scumbag
Scumbag, Scumbag
Scumbag, Scumbag

MIND GAMES

Mind Games
We're playing those mind games together
Pushing the barriers planting seeds
Playing the mind guerrilla
Chanting the Mantra peace on earth
We all been playing those mind games forever
Some kinda druid dudes lifting the veil
Doin' the mind guerrilla
Some call it magic, the search for the Grail

Love is the answer and you know that for sure
Love is a flower you got to let it, you got to let it grow

So keep on playing those mind games together
Faith in the future outta the now
You just can't beat on those mind guerrillas
Absolute elsewhere in the stones of your mind
Yeah we're playing those mind games forever
Projecting our images in space and in time

Yes is the answer and you know that for sure
Yes is surrender you got to let it, you got to let it go

So keep on playing those mind games together
Doing the ritual dance in the sun
Millions of mind guerrillas
Putting their soul power to the Karmic Wheel
Keep on playing those mind games forever
Raising the spirit of peace and love, love
(I want you to make love, not war, I know you've heard it before)

TIGHT A$

Just as tight a$ you can make it
Hard and slow ain't hard enough
Just as tight a$ you can shake it girl
Git it on and do your stuff

Tight a$ you can get it
Tight a$ got it made
Uptight's alright but if ya can't stand the heat
you better get back in the shade

Just as tight a$ an Indian rope trick
Long and tough ain't hard enough
Just as tight a$ a dope fiend's fix my friend
Git it up and do your stuff

Tight a$ you can boogie
Tight a$ got it made
Uptight's alright but if ya can't stand the heat
you better get back in the shade

Well tight a$ got me cornered
Tight a$ got me laid
Tight a$ strut your stuff so tough
Just a sweating in the midnight shade

Tight a$ you can boogie
Tight a$ got it made
Uptight's alright but if ya can't stand the heat
you better get back in the shade

AISUMASEN (I'M SORRY)

When I'm down really yin
And I don't know what I'm doing
Aisumasen aisumasen Yoko
All I had to do was call your name
All I had to do was call your name

And when I hurt you and cause you pain
Darlin' I promise I won't do it again
Aisumasen aisumasen Yoko
It's hard enough I know just to feel your own pain
It's hard enough I know just to feel your own pain
All that I know is just what you tell me
All that I know is just what you show me

When I'm down real sanpaku
And I don't know what to do
Aisumasen aisumasen Yoko san
All I had to do was call your name
Yes, all I had to do was call your name.

ONE DAY AT A TIME

You are my weakness, you are my strength
Nothing I have in the world makes better sense
Cause I'm the fish and you're the sea
When we're together or when we're apart
There's never a space between the beat of our hearts
Cause I'm the apple and you're the tree
One day at a time is all we do
One day at a time is good for you

You are my woman, I am your man
Nothing else matters at all, now I understand
That I'm the door and you're the key
And every morning I wake in your smile
Feeling your breath on my face and the love in your eyes
Cause you're the honey and I'm the bee
One day at a time is all we do
One day at a time is good for us two (you too).

BRING ON THE LUCIE (FREEDA PEEPLE)

We don't care what flag you're waving
We don't even want to know your name
We don't care where you're from or where you're going
All we know is that you came
You're making all our decisions
We have just one request of you
That while you're thinking things over
Here's something you just better do

Free the people now
Do it do it do it do it do it now

Well we were caught with our hands in the air
Don't despair, paranoia is everywhere
We can shake it with love when we're scared
So let's shout it aloud like a prayer

Free the people now
Do it do it do it do it do it now

We understand your paranoia
But we don't want to play your game
You think you're cool and know what you are doing
666 is your name
So while you're jerking off each other
You better bear this thought in mind
Your time is up you better know it
But maybe you don't read the signs

Free the people now
Do it do it do it do it do it now

Well you were caught with your hands in the kill
And you still got to swallow your pill
As you slip and you slide down the hill
On the blood of the people you killed

Stop the killing now
Do it do it do it do it do it now
Bring on the Lucie

INTUITION

My intentions are good, I use my intuition
It takes me for a ride
But I never understood other people's superstitions
It seemed like suicide
And as I play the game of life
I try to make it better each and every day
And when I struggle in the night
The magic of the music seems to light the way

Intuition takes me there
Intuition takes me everywhere

Well my instincts are fine
I had to learn to use them in order to survive
And time after time confirmed an old suspicion
It's good to be alive
And when I'm deep down and out and lose communication
With nothing left to say
It's then I realise it's only a condition
Of seeing things that way

Intuition takes me there
Intuition takes me anywhere

OUT THE BLUE

Out the blue you came to me
And blew away life's misery
Out the blue life's energy
Out the blue you came to me

Every day I thank the Lord and Lady
For the way that you came to me
Anyway it had to be two minds, one destiny

Out the blue you came to me
And blew away life's misery
Out the blue life's energy
Out the blue you came to me

All my life's been a long slow knife
I was born just to get to you
Anyway I survived long enough to make you my wife

Out the blue you came to me
And blew away life's misery
Out the blue life's energy
Out the blue you came to me

Like a UFO you came to me
And blew away life's misery
Out the blue life's energy
Out the blue you came to me

ONLY PEOPLE

Only people know just how to talk to people
Only people know just how to change the world
Only people realise the power of people
A million heads are better than one, so come on, get it on!

Well I know how we tried and the millions of tears that we cried
Now we are hipper we been thru the trip
And we can't be denied with woman and man side by side
Make no mistake it's our future we're making
Bake the cake and eat it too!
We don't want no pig brother scene!

Only people know just how to talk to people
Only people know just how to change the world
Only people realise the power of people
A million heads are better than one, so come on, get it on!

Well it's long overdue there ain't nothing better to do
Now we are hipper we been thru the trip
We can fly right on thru, there's nothing on earth we can't do
Fish or cut bait, it's our future we're making
All together now pull the chain!
We don't want no pig brother scene!

Only people know just how to talk to people
Only people know just how to change the world
Only people realise the power of people
A million heads are better than one, so come on, get it on!

I KNOW (I KNOW)

The years have passed so quickly
One thing I've understood
I am only learning
To tell the trees from the wood

I know what's coming down
And I know where it's coming from
And I know I'm sorry (yes I am)
But I never could speak my mind

And I know just how you feel
And I know now what I have done
And I know and I'm guilty (yes I am)
But I never could speak my mind

I know what I was missing
But now my eyes can see
I put myself in your place
As you did for me

Today I love you more than yesterday
Right now I love you more right now

Now I know what's coming down
I can feel where it's coming from
And I know it's getting better (all the time)
As we share in each other's minds

Today I love you more than yesterday
Right now I love you more right now
Ooh hoo no more crying
Ooh hoo no more crying.

YOU ARE HERE

From Liverpool to Tokyo
What a way to go
From distant lands one woman one man
Let the four winds blow

Three thousand miles over the ocean
Three thousand light years from the land of the rising sun
Love has opened up my eyes
Love has blown right through
Wherever you are, you are here
Wherever you are, you are here

Three thousand miles over the ocean
Three thousand light years from the surprising sun

East is east and west is west
The twain shall meet
East is west and west is east
Let it be complete

Three thousand miles over the ocean
Three thousand light years from the land of the morning star.

MEAT CITY

Well I been Meat City to see for myself
Yes I been Meat City to see for myself
Been Meat City been Meat City
Just got to give me some rock 'n' roll

People were dancing like there's no tomorrow

Meat City

Finger lickin' chickenpickin' Meat City shookdown USA

Well I been the mountain to see for myself
Yes I been the mountain to see for myself
Been the mountain, been the mountain
Just got to give me some rock 'n' roll

Snake doctors shakin' like there's no tomorrow
Freak City
Chickensuckin' mothertruckin' Meat City shookdown USA

Well I'm gonna China to see for myself
Well I'm gonna China to see for myself
Gonna China, gonna China
Just got to give me some rock'n'roll

Well the people were jumping like there's no tomorrow
Meat City
Chickensuckin' mothertruckin' Meat City shookdown USA

GOING DOWN ON LOVE

Got to get down, down on my knees
Got to get down, down on my knees
Going down on love
Going down on love
Going down, going down, going down
When the real thing goes wrong
And you can't get it on
And your love she has gone
And you got to carry on
And you shoot out the light
Ain't coming home for the night
You know you got to, got to, got to pay the price!

Somebody please, please help me
You know I'm drowning in a sea of hatred
Got to get down, down on my knees
Got to get down, down on my knees
Going down on love
Going down on love
Going down, going down, going down

Something precious and rare
Disappears in thin air
And it seems so unfair
Nothin' doin' nowhere
Well you burn all your boats
And you sow your wild oats

Well you know, you know, you know
The price is right!
Got to get down, down on my knees . . .

WHATEVER GETS YOU THROUGH THE NIGHT

Whatever gets you thru' the night
'salright, 'salright
It's your money or your life
'salright, 'salright
Don't need a sword to cut thru' flowers
Oh no, Oh no

Whatever gets you thru' your life
'salright, 'salright
Do it wrong or do it right
'sal right, 'sal right
Don't need a watch to waste your time
Oh no, Oh no

Hold me darlin', come on listen to me
I won't do you no harm
Trust me darlin', come on listen to me
come on listen to me, come on listen, listen

Whatever gets you to the light
'salright, 'salright
Out the blue or out of sight
'salright, 'salright
Don't need a gun to blow your mind
Oh no, oh no

OLD DIRT ROAD

Ain't no people on the old dirt road
No more weather on the old dirt road
But it's better than a mudslide mamma when the dry spell come
Oh oh oh old dirt road

Ain't no difference on the old dirt road
Tarred and feathered on the old dirt road
Trying to shovel smoke with a pitchfork in the wind
Breezing thru the deadwood on a hot summer day
I saw a human being lazybonin' out in the hay
I said uh, hey Mr. Human can ya rainmaker too?

He said I guess it's OK ya know the only thing we need is water
Cool, clear water!

Ain't no people on the old dirt road
No more weather on the old dirt road
But it's better than a mudslide mamma when the dry spell come
Oh oh oh old dirt road

WHAT YOU GOT

Don't wanna be a drag, everybody gotta bag
I know, I know, 'bout the emperor's clothes
You don't know what you got, until you lose it
You don't know what you got, until you lose it
You don't know what you got, until you lose it
Oh baby, baby, baby gimme one more chance

Well it's Saturday night and I just gotta rip it up
Sunday morning I just gotta give it up
Come Monday momma and I just gotta run away
You know it's such a drag to face another day
You don't know what you got, until you lose it
You don't know what you got, until you lose it
You don't know what you got, until you lose it
Oh baby, baby, baby gimme one more chance

You know the more it change, the more it stays the same
You gotta hang on in, you gotta cut the string
You don't know what you got, until you lose it

BLESS YOU

Bless you wherever you are
Windswept child on a shooting star
Restless spirits depart
Still we're deep in each other's hearts

Some people say it's over
Now that we spread our wings
But we know better darling
The hollow ring is only last year's echo

Bless you whoever you are
Holding her now
Be warm and kind hearted
Remember altho love is strange
Now and forever our love will remain

SCARED

I'm scared, I'm scared, I'm scared, I'm scared, so scared
I'm scared, I'm scared, I'm scared
As the years roll away
And the price that I paid
As the straw slips away
You don't have to suffer
It is what it is
No bell book or candle
Can get you out of this oh no!

I'm scarred, I'm scarred, I'm scarred, I'm scarred
I'm scarred, I'm scarred, I'm scarred
Every day of my life
I just manage to survive
I just wanna stay alive
You don't have to worry
In heaven or hell
Just dance to the music
You do it so well, well, well

Hatred and jealousy, gonna be the death of me
I guess I knew it right from the start
Sing out about love and peace
Don't wanna see the red raw meat
The green eyed goddam straight from your heart

I'm tired, I'm tired I'm tired
Of being so alone
No place to call my own
Like a rollin' stone

#9 DREAM

So long ago
Was it in a dream? Was it just a dream?
I know, yes I know
It seemed so very real, it seemed so real to me
Took a walk down the street
Thru the heat whispered trees
I thought I could hear (hear, hear, hear)
Somebody call out my name as it started to rain
Two spirits dancing so strange

Ah! bowakawa pousse, pousse
Ah! bowakawa pousse, pousse
Ah! bowakawa pousse, pousse

Dream, dream away
Magic in the air, was magic in the air?
I believe, yes I believe
More I cannot say, what more can I say?

On a river of sound
Thru the mirror go round, round
I thought I could feel (feel, feel, feel)
Music touching my soul, something warm, sudden cold
The spirit dance was unfolding

Ah! bowakawa pousse, pousse

SURPRISE, SURPRISE (SWEET BIRD OF PARADOX)

Sweet as the smell of success
Her body's warm and wet
She gets me thru this God awful loneliness
A natural high a butterfly Oh I
I need, need, need her

Just like a willow tree
a breath of spring you see
And Oh boy you don't know what she do to me
She makes me sweat and forget who I am
I need, need, need, need her

Well, I was wondering how long this could go on, on and on
I thought I could never be surprised
But could it be that I bit my own tongue
It's so hard to swallow when you're wrong

A bird of paradise
Sunrise in her eyes
God only knows such a sweet surprise
I was blind, she blew my mind think that I
I love, love, love, love her

STEEL AND GLASS

This is a story about your friend and mine!

There you stand with your L.A. tan
And your New York Walk and your New York talk
Your mother left you when you were small
But you're gonna wish you wasn't born at all
Steel and glass
Steel and glass

Your phone don't ring, no one answers your call
How does it feel to be off the wall?
Your mouthpiece squawks as you spread your lies
But you can't pull strings if your hands are tied

Your teeth are clean but your mind is capped
You leave your smell like an alley cat
Steel and glass
Steel and glass

Nobody Loves You When You're Down and Out

Nobody loves you when you're down and out
Nobody sees you when you're on cloud nine
Everybody's hustlin' for a buck and a dime
I'll scratch your back and you scratch mine

I've been across to the other side
I've shown you everything, I got nothing to hide
But still you ask me do I love you, what it is, what it is?
All I can tell you is it's all show biz
All I can tell you is it's all show biz

Nobody loves you when you're down and out
Nobody sees you when you're on cloud nine
Everybody's hustlin' for a buck and a dime
I'll scratch your back and you knife mine

I've been across the water now so many times
I've seen the one-eyed witchdoctor leading the blind
But still you ask me do I love you, what you say, what you say
Everytime I put my finger on it, it slips away
Everytime I put my finger on it, it slips away

Well I get up in the morning and I'm looking in the mirror to see, ooo wee!
Then I'm lying in the darkness and I know I can't get to sleep, ooo wee!

Nobody loves you when you're old and grey
Nobody needs you when you're upside down
Everybody's hollerin' 'bout their own birthday
Everybody loves you when you're six foot in the ground

his Glamour

(JUST LIKE) STARTING OVER

Our life together is so precious together
We have grown - we have grown
Although our love is still special
Let's take a chance and fly away somewhere alone

It's been too long since we took the time
No-one's to blame, I know time flies so quickly
But when I see you darling
It's like we both are falling in love again
It'll be like starting over - starting over

Everyday we used to make it love
Why can't we be making love nice and easy
It's time to spread our wings and fly
Don't let another day go by my love
It'll be just like starting over - starting over

Why don't we take off alone
Take a trip somewhere far, far away
We'll be together on our own again
Like we used to in the early days
Well, well, well darling

Our life together is so precious together
We have grown - we have grown
Although our love is still special
Let's take a chance and fly away somewhere alone

It's been too long since we took the time
No-one's to blame, I know time flies so quickly
But when I see you darling
It's like we both are falling in love again
It'll be like starting over - starting over

CLEANUP TIME

Moonlight on the water
Sunlight on my face
You and me together
We are in our place
The gods are in the heavens
The angels treat us well
The oracle has spoken
We cast the (perfect) spell

Now it begins - let it begin
Cleanup time
(Show those mothers how to do it)

The queen is in the counting house
Counting out the money
The king is in the kitchen
Making bread and honey
No friends and yet no enemies
Absolutely free
No rats aboard the magic ship
Of (perfect) harmony

Now it begins - let it begin
Cleanup time
(Show those mothers how to do it)

However far we travel
Wherever we may roam
The centre of the circle
Will always be our home
The gods are in the heaven
The angels treat us well
The oracle has spoken
We cast the (perfect) spell

DEAR YOKO

Even after all these years
I miss you when you're not here
I wish you were here today dear Yoko
Even if it's just a day
I miss you when you're away
I wish you were here today dear Yoko

Even if it's just one night
I miss you and it don't feel right
I wish you were here tonight dear Yoko
Even if it's just an hour
I wilt like a fading flower
Ain't nothing in the world like our love dear Yoko
Oh Yoko
I'll never ever let you go

Even when I'm miles at sea
And nowhere is the place to be
Your spirit's watching over me dear Yoko
Even when I watch TV
There's a hole where you're supposed to be
There's nobody lying next to me
Oh Yoko
I'll never ever let you go

Even after all this time
I miss you like the sun don't shine
Without you I'm a one track mind dear Yoko
After all is really said and done
The two of us are really one
The goddess really smiled upon our love dear Yoko

I'M LOSING YOU

Here in some stranger's room
Late in the afternoon
What am I doing here at all?
Ain't no doubt about it

I'm losing you
Somehow the wires have crossed
Communication's lost
Can't even get you on the telephone
Just got to shout about it
I'm losing you

Here in the Valley of Indecision
I don't know what to do
I feel you slipping away
I feel you slipping away
I'm losing you
I'm losing you

You say you're not getting enough
But I remind you of all that bad bad stuff
So what the hell am I supposed to do?
Just put a bandaid on it?
And stop the bleeding now
Stop the bleeding now

I know I hurt you then
But hell that was way back when
And well, do you still have to carry that cross?
Don't want to hear about it
I'm losing you
I'm losing you

BEAUTIFUL BOY (DARLING BOY)

Close your eyes
Have no fear
The monster's gone
He's on the run and your daddy's here
Beautiful
Beautiful beautiful
Beautiful Boy

Before you go to sleep
Say a little prayer
Every day in every way
It's getting better and better
Beautiful
Beautiful beautiful
Beautiful boy

Out on the ocean sailing away
I can hardly wait
To see you come of age
But I guess we'll both
Just have to be patient
It's a long way to go
But in the meantime

Before you cross the street
Take my hand
Life is what happens to you
While you're busy
Making other plans

Beautiful
Beautiful
Beautiful boy
Darling
Darling
Darling Sean

WATCHING THE WHEELS

People say I'm crazy doing what I'm doing
Well they give me all kinds of warnings to save me from ruin
When I say that I'm OK they look at me kind of strange
Surely you're not happy now you no longer play the game
People say I'm lazy dreaming my life away
Well they give me all kinds of advice designed to enlighten me
When I tell them that I'm doing fine watching shadows on the wall
Don't you miss the big time boy you're no longer on the ball?

I'm just sitting here watching the wheels go round and round
I really love to watch them roll
No longer riding on the merry-go-round
I just had to let it go

People asking questions lost in confusion
Well I tell them there's no problem, only solutions
Well they shake their heads and look at me as if I've lost my mind
I tell them there's no hurry . . .
I'm just sitting here doing time

I'm just sitting here watching the wheels go round and round
I really love to watch them roll
No longer riding on the merry-go-round
I just had to let it go

WOMAN

Woman
I can hardly express
My mixed emotion at my thoughtlessness
After all I'm forever in your debt
And woman I will try to express
My inner feelings and thankfulness
For showing me the meaning of success ooh well
Woman I know you understand
The little child inside the man
Please remember my life is in your hands
And woman hold me close to your heart
However distant don't keep us apart
After all it is written in the stars ooh well
Woman please let me explain
I never mean(t) to cause you sorrow or pain
So let me tell you again and again and again
(I love you now and forever)